Puerto Rico

Jim Ollhoff

Visit us at
www.abdopublishing.com

Published by ABDO Publishing Company, 8000 West 78th Street, Suite 310, Edina, Minnesota 55439 USA. Copyright ©2010 by Abdo Consulting Group, Inc. International copyrights reserved in all countries. No part of this book may be reproduced in any form without written permission from the publisher. The Checkerboard Library™ is a trademark and logo of ABDO Publishing Company.

Printed in the United States.

Editor: John Hamilton
Graphic Design: Sue Hamilton
Cover Illustration: Neil Klinepier
Cover Photo: iStock Photo
Interior Photo Credits: AirPhoto-Jim Wark, Alamy, AP Images, Brendon.M, Corbis, Getty, iStock Photo, Jupiterimages, Lev Frid, Library of Congress, Mile High Maps, Mountain High Maps, One Mile Up, Peter Arnold Inc, Puerto Rico Tsunami Warning and Mitigation Program, RavenFire Media, and Roosevelt Roads Naval Base.
Statistics: Commonwealth population statistics taken from 2008 U.S. Census Bureau estimates. City and town population statistics taken from 2007 American Community Servey 1-Year Estimates, U.S. Census Bureau. Land and water area statistics taken from 2000 Census, U.S. Census Bureau.

Manufactured with paper containing at least 10% post-consumer waste

Library of Congress Cataloging-in-Publication Data

Ollhoff, Jim, 1959-
  Puerto Rico / Jim Ollhoff.
     p. cm. -- (The United States)
  Includes index.
  ISBN 978-1-60453-674-4
  1. Puerto Rico--Juvenile literature. I. Title.

F1958.3.O45 2010
972.95--dc22
                                   2008052398

Table of Contents

Island of Enchantment

Puerto Rico is not a state of the United States. The island's official name is the "Commonwealth of Puerto Rico." This means that Puerto Rico is a self-governing part of the United States, but it is not a state. The Puerto Rican government can make its own local laws, but the United States government can step in if needed. Puerto Ricans are considered U.S. citizens, but they can't vote in presidential elections.

Puerto Rico's nickname is the Island of Enchantment. The colorful scenery and tropical climate make it a popular vacation spot. Its mix of cultures and interesting history makes the island a unique place to visit. With nightclubs, art museums, forest-covered mountains, and sandy beaches, Puerto Rico is always enchanting.

Puerto Rico is an island of beauty. Many visitors come to see its beaches, cities, and rain forest.

Quick Facts

Name: Puerto Rico is a Spanish term meaning "rich port."

Capital: San Juan

Date of Commonwealth: July 25, 1952

Population: 3,954,037

Area (Total Land and Water): 5,324 sq mi (13,789 sq km)

Largest City: San Juan; population 411,384

Nickname: Island of Enchantment

Motto: *Joannes est nomen ejus* (John is thy name)

National Bird: Stripe-Headed Tanager

National Flower: Puerto Rican Hibiscus

National Tree: Kapok

National Song: "The Borinquen Anthem" ("La Borinqueña")

Highest Point: 4,393 ft (1,339 m), Cerro de Punta

Lowest Point: 0 ft (0 m), Caribbean Sea

Average July Temperature: 83°F (28°C)

Record High Temperature: 103° F (39°C) at San Lorenzo, August 22, 1906

Cerro de Punta

Average January Temperature: 77°F (25°C)

Record Low Temperature: 40°F (4°C) at Aibonito, March 9, 1911

Average Annual Precipitation: 46 in (117 cm)

Number of U.S. Senators: Zero

Number of U.S. Representatives: Zero

Caribbean Sea

U.S. Postal Service Abbreviation: PR

Geography

The Commonwealth of Puerto Rico is a set of islands about 1,000 miles (1,609 km) southeast of Florida. The main island is called Puerto Rico. There are also several smaller islands, including Culebra, Mona, Desecheo, and Vieques.

Puerto Rico is about 110 miles (177 km) across, from east to west. From north to south, the island measures about 39 miles (63 km).

To the north of Puerto Rico is the Atlantic Ocean. On the east side of the island is a body of water called the Virgin Passage. The Virgin Islands are farther east. On the south side of the island is the Caribbean Sea. To the west is an island called the Dominican Republic, separated by a body of water called the Mona Passage.

ATLANTIC OCEAN

N

0   40 miles
0   40 km

San Juan   Carolina

Bayamőn

MONA PASSAGE

Ponce

PUERTO RICO

CARIBBEAN SEA

The island of Puerto Rico is in the Caribbean Sea. Puerto Rico's total land and water area is 5,324 square miles (13,789 sq km). The capital and largest city is San Juan.

Puerto Rico has four main areas of land. The Coastal Lowlands form a narrow strip along the north and south coasts of the island. Most of Puerto Rico's larger cities are located here. The Coastal Valleys are along the east and west ends of the island. Sugarcane and other crops are grown here. The Foothills and the Central Mountains run east and west across the island. Coffee is a major crop grown in the fertile valleys of the mountain areas.

Sunrise over an agricultural valley in Puerto Rico.

Puerto Rico has 17 man-made lakes. There are more than 50 rivers and streams. Some rivers have been dammed to make hydroelectric power.

The Carraízo Lake Dam in Trujillo Alto, Puerto Rico. The Carraízo hydroelectric dam was built in 1953-1954.

Climate and Weather

The temperature of Puerto Rico averages about 80 degrees Fahrenheit (27°C) throughout the year. There is not much change in the seasons. Winds come from the northeast, off the ocean. This brings a lot of warm air.

Puerto Rico has mostly warm, breezy days.

The northeast winds from the ocean also bring a lot of water vapor. When the water vapor is pushed up the mountains, it gets cooler. This makes the water vapor condense, and it rains. Some of the mountain areas get more than 200 inches (508 cm) of rain each year. Rainfall varies widely across the island.

Puerto Rico is sometimes hit by hurricanes that form in the Atlantic Ocean. The hurricane season is from June to November.

The entire island of Puerto Rico was hit by 110 mile-per-hour (177 kilometer-per-hour) winds and heavy rain when Hurricane Georges came ashore in 1998. Thousands of people were left without clean water or electricity for many days.

Plants and Animals

Puerto Rico is rich in plants and vegetation. The north side of the island is a tropical rain forest. The forests are full of brightly colored plants and flowers.

Puerto Rico was once heavily forested. By the early 1900s, much of the forest was cut down. In the 1930s, the government started a tree replanting effort. Along with native trees, they brought in hardwoods such as mahogany, laurel, and ebony. Today there are a variety of trees and tropical shrubs. Poinciana, kopok, bougainvillea, sierra and coconut palm, breadfruit, and tree fern are found on the island. To the southwest, in parts of the island with less rainfall, cactus and bunch grass are found.

Breadfruit

A hiker explores a cavern in a tropical rain forest in the northern part of Puerto Rico. A wide variety of trees, flowers, and plants grow in this rich, rainy area.

There are no large wild animals on the island. In the 1800s, farmers brought mongooses to the island to help control rats in the sugarcane fields. However, most of the mongooses preferred eating birds instead of rats. Today, mongooses can be found all over the island.

Mongooses on Puerto Rico prefer to eat birds and their eggs.

There are more than 60 types of reptiles on Puerto Rico, including turtles, snakes, and lizards. There are more than 25 types of amphibians. One of the more famous frogs is the common coqui. Puerto Rico is one of the only places in the world where the coqui lives.

Dolphin, barracuda, tuna, mullet, lobster, and oyster are some of the marine animals living in the waters around Puerto Rico.

A coqui is tiny. The singing tree frog is small enough to fit on the tip of a finger.

Barracuda

Puerto Rican Parrot

Iguana

History

The first inhabitants of Puerto Rico lived on the island as early as 2000 BC. The Igneri tribe replaced those first people before 400 AD. Then, sometime between 700 and 1100 AD, the Taíno people arrived. The Taíno may have come by boat from South America. The Taíno lived on many of the islands in the Caribbean.

A sculpture of a Taíno man. The Taíno may have come by boat from South America. They inhabited Puerto Rico and many other islands in the area.

A statue of Christopher Columbus in San Juan, Puerto Rico.

In 1493, Christopher Columbus landed on the island. He declared that Spain owned the land, even though thousands of Taíno lived there. Columbus named the island *San Juan Bautista*, for St. John the Baptist from the Bible. Later, the biggest city became known as San Juan. The name Puerto Rico, which means "rich port," referred only to the port of San Juan. Over time, the name Puerto Rico began to refer to the whole island.

In 1508, a Spaniard named Juan Ponce de Leon invaded Puerto Rico. He became governor of the island in 1509. The Taíno died from disease, warfare, and mistreatment. Soon, the Spanish began to bring African slaves to the island to work the large farms and plantations.

Juan Ponce de Leon

The 1500s, 1600s, and 1700s were tough times in Puerto Rico. Pirates harassed the people. The English, French, and Dutch raided cities. Indian tribes from neighboring islands raided the farms and plantations. In order to protect the towns from raids, the Spanish built large forts. Near San Juan Harbor, they built San Felipe del Morro Castle. Later, they built a larger fort called San Cristóbal. Many parts of these forts are still standing today.

By the 1830s, Puerto Rico was a thriving agricultural island. Huge farms called plantations grew sugarcane and coffee. The work on these plantations was mostly done by slave labor.

A view of the inside and the outside of San Felipe del Morro Castle near San Juan Harbor.

In 1898, Spain and the United States fought a war called the Spanish-American War. The war ended with the United States getting control of several Caribbean islands, including Puerto Rico. The United States formed a government on the island. In 1917, Puerto Ricans were able to become U.S. citizens.

In 1898, American warships fired at Spanish ships and on San Felipe del Morro Castle at San Juan, Puerto Rico.

During World War II, the United States military constructed an important naval base in San Juan. After the war, Puerto Ricans worked to get more manufacturing to the island. This helped the economy.

Some Puerto Ricans wanted to be independent of the United States. Others wanted to become the 51st state. Others found a middle ground. They wanted to become a commonwealth, or territory, of the U.S. Sometimes the discussion of how to relate to the United States became violent. But in 1952, a majority of voters decided that Puerto Rico should become a commonwealth of the United States.

On July 22, 1952, a parade celebrated Puerto Rico's new constitution, which established the island as a commonwealth.

Did You Know?

Some people in Puerto Rico continue to want the island to become the 51st state of the United States. They

Many people want Puerto Rico to become a state, but the voters have kept it a commonwealth.

say that becoming a state will bring more business to the island. They say that statehood will bring government help to build bridges, roads, and schools. Becoming a state means having representatives in Congress.

Others say that statehood will be expensive. They say the cost of living will rise. They say that statehood will make the culture of the island more like the United States. Puerto Ricans like their unique identity and colorful mix of heritages.

Puerto Ricans have voted on the issue several times. Each time, voters decided by a small margin to remain a U.S. commonwealth.

Earthquakes sometimes strike Puerto Rico. A very bad earthquake occurred in 1918. The earthquake triggered a tsunami, which slammed into the island's northwest coast. More than 100 people died, and many buildings, bridges, and roads were destroyed.

People

Roberto Clemente

(1934–1972) was born in the Puerto Rican city of Carolina. He started playing baseball at a young age. In 1954, the Pittsburgh Pirates drafted him to play professional baseball. He was one of the best outfielders to play the game, winning 12 Gold Glove awards. He was the league's Most Valuable Player in 1966. In 1972, there was an earthquake in Nicaragua. He wanted to help, so he went on an airplane loaded with supplies. Tragically, the airplane crashed, ending his life. Major League Baseball honored him by inducting him to the Hall of Fame in 1973.

Roselyn Sánchez

(1973–) is a singer, model, writer, and actress. She was born in San Juan. She moved to New York City when she was 18. She took classes in acting and dancing. After working as a model, she started acting in movies, including the *Rush Hour 2*. In 2005, she joined the cast of the TV show *Without A Trace*. She is also the spokesperson for a group that helps sick children.

Agüeybaná (?–1510) was a powerful chief of the Taíno people. He was the chief when the first Spaniards arrived on the island in 1493, and again in 1508. He welcomed Juan Ponce de Leon,

Juan Ponce de Leon was first welcomed by Chief Agüeybaná.

and wanted friendly relations with the Spanish. He helped the Spanish explore the island. Unfortunately, the Spanish took over the island, and then forced the Taíno people into slave labor. After Chief Agüeybaná's death, his brother led a revolt against the Spanish. The Spanish had guns, and easily defeated the revolt. Agüeybaná's brother died in 1511.

Ricky Martin (1971-) is a Grammy Award-winning pop singer. He was born in Hato Rey, Puerto Rico. His real name is Enrique Martín Morales. At age 13, he became part of the popular boy-band Menudo, which was composed of young Puerto Rican musicians. He left the band at age 17, finished high school, and then began a solo singing career. He has sold more than 55 million albums worldwide.

Cities

San Juan is the capital and the most important city in Puerto Rico. Founded by the Spanish conquistador Juan Ponce de Leon in 1508, San Juan is one of the oldest cities in the western hemisphere. In the 1530s, the Spanish began constructing massive forts to protect themselves from pirates, Indians, and European military attacks. These forts and many old historic buildings are still standing. Today, San Juan is the manufacturing and business center of the island. Factories make sugar, chemicals, clothing, and other items. San Juan is the home of several colleges, including the University of Puerto Rico. The city's population is 411,384.

Just to the southwest of San Juan is the city of **Bayamón**. It was established in 1772. The name might have come from the Taíno name of a river in the area. Some historians say the name came from a Taíno chief. Today, the city has factories that manufacture automobile parts, furniture, food, and other household goods. It is home to Bayamón Central University. The city's population is about 201,457.

Just to the southeast of San Juan is the city of **Carolina**. It is part of the metropolitan area that includes Bayamón, Guaynabo, Toa Baja, and San Juan. The city was founded in 1816, and named after the king of Spain. The city has many manufacturing factories and is a popular tourist destination. Carolina's population is about 171,525.

On the southern side of Puerto Rico is the city of **Ponce**. It was founded in the 1670s. It was named after the grandson of Spanish conquistador Ponce de Leon. With a population of about 150,833, it is the largest city outside the San Juan metropolitan area. The city has many historic Spanish buildings, but also is a manufacturing center.

Transportation

San Juan is Puerto Rico's leading port for ships. The busiest airport on the island is in the San Juan metropolitan

About 11 million passengers use Luis Muñoz Marín International Airport each year.

area. Luis Muñoz Marín International Airport is one of the main airports for islands in the Caribbean. It is located in Carolina, a city in the San Juan metropolitan area. The cities of Aguadilla, Ponce, and Mayaguez also have airports. There are more than 25 airports on the island, but many of them are very small.

A system of highways circles Puerto Rico near the coast. There are about 12,020 miles (19,344 km) of roads on the island. Most of them are paved. There are also railroad tracks on the island. Most of the railroads are for hauling sugarcane.

A Puerto Rican highway cuts through limestone cliffs. Puerto Rico has a system of highways that circle the island near the coast.

Natural Resources

Puerto Rico has small amounts of minerals that can be mined. Limestone, clay, cobalt, nickel, and iron ore are found on the island. There are large amounts of copper in the center of the island.

There are two kinds of farms on Puerto Rico. Most are very small, and the crops are sold locally. There are also very large farms that grow crops that are sold in the United States and other places. The main crops are coffee, vegetables, sugarcane, and bananas. Some farmers raise cattle and poultry.

Commercial fishing and fish farming are a small part of the economy. Bass, tuna, bluegill, and catfish are raised and then sold to restaurants on the island and in the United States.

A coffee bean farmer picks ripened beans on a farm in Puerto Rico. Coffee is one of the main crops of the island.

Industry

For most of Puerto Rico's history, the economy has not been as strong as that of the United States. In the 1940s, the government worked hard to attract manufacturing companies. This has helped the island's economy.

Storage tanks hold chemicals at a manufacturing company in Puerto Rico.

Manufacturing today is the main part of Puerto Rico's economy. Chemicals, food, electronic equipment, and clothes are the main products that are manufactured on the island.

Tourists visit San Felipe del Morro Castle near San Juan.

Tourism is a big part of the economy. About five million people visit the island each year.

Although agriculture is important, it is a small part of Puerto Rico's overall economy.

Sports

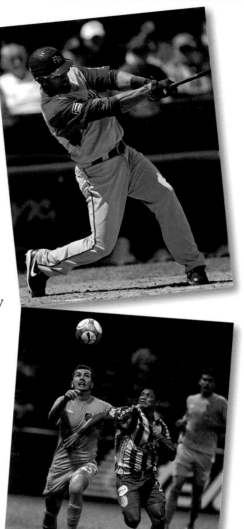

Baseball is the most popular sport in Puerto Rico. Many Puerto Rican baseball players have become players in Major League Baseball in the United States. Also, many people play in island leagues and clubs.

Soccer, boxing, golf, and basketball are also popular. Many clubs and franchises play against each other.

The Puerto Rican National Baseball Team and the Puerto Rico Islanders are popular sports teams.

Puerto Rico is known for its beautiful beaches.

Puerto Rico sends many athletes to the Summer and Winter Olympic Games. Athletes from the island have won several Olympic medals.

Puerto Rico is famous for its sandy beaches. It is a good place for swimming, surfing, boating, and fishing. The warm weather makes Puerto Rico a good place for playing tennis and golf. Horseracing is also popular.

Entertainment

Music and dance are very important to the people of Puerto Rico. Some songs and dances are based on Spanish and African songs. Island musicians influenced the musical styles of Latin jazz and salsa. Ballet and other dance companies are common. Opera and classical music are performed throughout the year. San Juan is the center of many artistic activities.

Puerto Rico was once a Spanish colony. Many of the island's buildings still have a Spanish design. The oldest part of the city of San Juan has huge fortresses that were built by the Spanish. San Felipe del Morro and San Cristóbal are two of the forts that were built in the early 1500s. Today, millions of visitors each year enjoy exploring these historic fortresses.

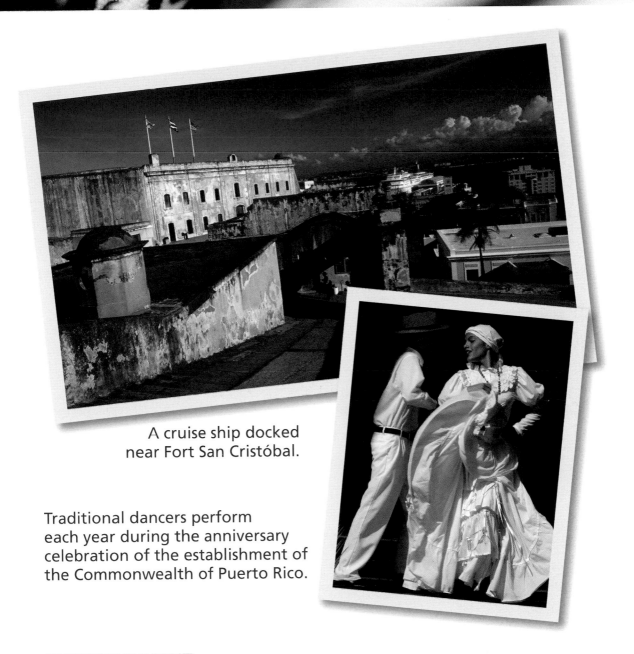

A cruise ship docked
near Fort San Cristóbal.

Traditional dancers perform
each year during the anniversary
celebration of the establishment of
the Commonwealth of Puerto Rico.

Timeline

2000 BC—The first inhabitants of Puerto Rico arrive on the island.

1100—The Taíno people arrive from South America.

1493—Columbus lands on Puerto Rico.

1508-1509—Juan Ponce de Leon, a Spanish conquistador, invades Puerto Rico and becomes the island's governor.

1500s—The forts of San Felipe del Morro Castle and San Cristóbal are built.

 **1898**—Spain and the United States fight the Spanish-American War. The United States gets control of Puerto Rico.

 **1917**—Puerto Ricans are able to become United States citizens.

 **1941-1945**—American involvement in World War II. The United States builds an important naval base in San Juan.

 **1952**—Puerto Ricans vote to become a commonwealth of the United States.

 **2003**—Because of protests, the United States Navy stops airplane bombing training on Vieques, a small island east of the main island of Puerto Rico.

Glossary

Breadfruit—A starchy fruit often cooked or used in place of flour.

Caribbean—An area of the Atlantic Ocean south of Puerto Rico and north of South America.

Commonwealth—A self-governing territory that is voluntarily part of another country. Puerto Rico is a commonwealth of the United States. Although not an official state, Puerto Ricans are citizens of the U.S.

Conquistador—A Spanish military conqueror or adventurer of the 1500s.

Hydroelectric Power—When rivers are dammed, a controlled flow of water runs turbines, which drive generators that create electricity.

Plantation—A large farm where cash crops such as coffee, sugar, or tobacco are raised by people who live on the estate. In Puerto Rico's early history, African slaves worked on large sugarcane and coffee plantations.

Salsa—A kind of Latin American dance music. Salsa is a fusion of jazz and rock. The term also refers to the dance that is performed to salsa music.

Spanish-American War—A war started in April 1898 between Spain and the United States. The war was fought to help the islands of Puerto Rico, Cuba, and the Philippeans gain freedom from Spain. The war ended in December 1898 with Spain giving up the islands by signing the Treaty of Paris.

Tsunami—A large sea wave that is created by earthquakes or underwater landslides. When tsunamis strike land, they can be very destructive.

Index

A
Aguadilla, PR 34
Agüeybaná 28
Atlantic Ocean 8, 12

B
Bayamón, PR 31, 32
Bayamón Central
  University 31
Bible 19

C
Caribbean Sea 8, 18,
  22, 34
Carolina, PR 26, 32,
  34
Central Mountains 10
Clemente, Roberto
  26
Coastal Lowlands 10
Coastal Valleys 10
Columbus,
  Christopher 19
Commonwealth of
  Puerto Rico 4, 8
Congress, U.S. 24
Culebra 8

D
Desecheo 8
Dominican Republic
  8

F
Florida 8
Foothills 10

G
Gold Glove Award 26
Grammy Award 29
Guaynabo, PR 32

H
Hall of Fame 26
Hato Rey, PR 29

I
Igneri (tribe) 18

J
John the Baptist,
  Saint 19

L
Luis Muñoz Marín
  International
  Airport 34

M
Major League Baseball
  26, 40
Martin, Ricky 29
Mayaguez, PR 34
Menudo 29
Mona 8
Mona Passage 8
Morales, Enrique
  Martín 29

N
New York, NY 27
Nicaragua 26

O
Olympic Games 41

P
Pittsburgh Pirates 26
Ponce, PR 33, 34
Ponce de Leon, Juan
  20, 28, 30, 33
Puerto Rico (port) 19

R
Rush Hour 2 27

S
San Cristóbal 21, 42
San Felipe del Morro
  Castle 20, 42
San Juan, PR 19, 23,
  27, 30, 31, 32, 33,
  34, 42
San Juan Bautista 19
San Juan Harbor 20
Sánchez, Roselyn 27
South America 18
Spain 19, 22, 32
Spanish-American
  War 22

T
Taíno (tribe) 18, 19,
  20, 28, 31
Toa Baja, PR 32

U
United States 4, 22,
  23, 24, 25, 36, 38,
  40
University of Puerto
  Rico 30

V
Vieques 8
Virgin Islands 8
Virgin Passage 8

W
Without a Trace 27
World War II 23